NADIA WALKER

# Top 10 Things To Do In Saint Martin

## THE MUST DO LIST

# Contents

# 1

# Introduction

I wanted to write this book as this was the guidebook I WISHED I had when I visited. I went through a lot of YouTube videos and articles on what to do when I got to Saint Martin, but honestly, they all missed the mark for me. It felt like most of them were written from a purely promotional standpoint versus a more discerning vantage. So here we are and why I decided to write this guidebook.

I am, by all definitions, an AVID traveler. I have visited about 30 different countries and done the full range of super budget (college and young adult) to luxe. I had the wanderlust bug for as long as I can remember and still to this day it is one of my biggest life passions. I am also a planner when it comes to traveling. Although I like a certain amount of spontaneous and "go with the flow" vibe, when it comes to getting the most out of my cherished vacations, I want to make sure I get as much joy out of these moments as possible. Sure, some things will go haywire at times, but if you leave too much up to "being spontaneous," then I have found from my experience...it is a headache. So, I have included the BEST THINGS to do in St. Martin so you can avoid these types of headaches.

One year, I decided to "live a year without fear." If I really wanted to do something, I was going to figure out how to make it happen. I live in New York City, and as you can imagine, although the city has amazing pluses, calm, nature and serenity isn't one of them. Central Park is one of the world's greatest park experiences, but there are only so many weekends you can run around the same loop, walk on the trails, and picnic on the same lawns. I have been living in NYC for over 25+ years, so I take as many chances as possible to get out of dodge and try to grab as much nature and calm as possible.

One day, I decided to live somewhere warm and tropical for about a month but out of the country. I was looking at someplace with roughly the same time zone, where I could walk out and be right on the beach. After weeks of looking at places and keeping in mind budget, access to extremely reliable WiFi (as I needed to work remotely), and other "livable" topics, I narrowed it down to Saint Martin. I booked my Airbnb and started the journey of living on the beach.

# 2

# Some Background

Like much of the Caribbean, it is an interesting mix of indigenous cultures and European Colonial powers.

Saint Martin was originally inhabited by the Arawaks, who arrived in the area around 1000 AD. They were known for living a very peaceful lifestyle and agricultural practices. They were skilled farmers, fishermen, and artisans. Arawaks were believed to have originated from South America, migrating through the Lesser Antilles to various parts of the Caribbean (including, of course, Saint Martin). They navigated in canoes and spread their culture and agriculture practices across the Caribbean before the arrival of the Europeans.

The Caribs arrived in the 15th century, much later than the Arawaks. The Caribs also arrived from South America but from the northeastern end, around the regions today Venezuela and possibly parts of the Guyanas. They expanded throughout the Caribbean, moving northward into the Lesser Antilles and other islands, displacing the Arawaks and establishing themselves as the dominant culture in many areas before European contact. The Caribs were more aggressive and warlike than the Arawaks, known for their prowess in warfare and navigation. Their arrival marked significant changes in the Caribbean's indigenous cultures, often leading to conflicts with the Arawaks and later with European colonizers.

SIDEBAR: Why is the Lesser Antilles called the Lesser Antilles? The region is called "Lesser," not due to their importance but because of their smaller size compared to the larger islands in the Caribbean, known as the Greater Antilles. This geographical term helps to distinguish between the two groups of islands based on their size and location in the eastern Caribbean Sea. I throw this out there because I often wonder how things/places got their names, in case you tend to be on the super curious side.

The European influence on the island began with Christopher Columbus, who claimed the island for Spain in 1493. However, the Spanish did not colonize it. In the 17th century, the French and Dutch established settlements attracted by salt deposits. The island's strategic location and resources led to numerous conflicts between these European powers, culminating in the 1648 Treaty of Concordia, which divided Saint Martin between France and the Netherlands. This division introduced and solidified European cultural influences, shaping the island's architecture, cuisine, languages, and customs.

After Europeans arrived in the Caribbean, the indigenous populations of the Caribs and Arawaks faced significant decline due to diseases brought by Europeans, warfare, and enslavement, like much of the Caribbean. Their numbers drastically reduced, and their cultures were significantly altered or absorbed into the colonial societies established by European powers.

## HURRICANE IRMA  Sept. 2017

There is Saint Martin pre-Irma and post-Irma. Hurricane Irma was the worst hurricane to hit the island in modern history. About 70% of the houses were destroyed, 90% of the buildings were damaged, and 95% of the French side was destroyed.

Even six years later, the island hasn't really been built back to it's former glory. This is not to take away from the general warmness of the people of the island and the natural beauty but there is still a lot that should be done for the island to live up to its full potential. When I went through "tourist" books, blogs and Youtube videos, this issue was not really addressed so this is one of the reasons why I wanted to make this book more "real" for the reader. This was one of the more shocking things I saw when I was visiting Saint Martin and it made me very sad for this island. Although there has been good progress on the rebuild, much of the island is still dilapidated. Parts of the island look like a war zone. With many inhabitants not making a lot of money, many simply couldn't afford to rebuild to what it was before the hurricane. There are promises from both the Dutch and French sides to rebuild, but the progress has been ungodly slow from what I can tell. I personally don't think Saint Martin is a priority of either parent government but my hope is that this improves in the coming years. There is so much potential for this island to be stunning, given the beautiful water, the location, and the people.

## THE AIRPORT

I thought this should be under "The Basics" chapter, but after some thought, I felt it should be in this chapter. I have traveled through Saint Martin numerous times to St. Barths and couldn't wait to get out of this airport. For many years, it looked like a cardboard box, filled with noisy construction and makeshift everything.

Now, I am very happy to see a beautiful brand new airport that rivals many of the new airports in the world. It is clean, shiny, and filled with lots of great shops and restaurants. Coming from New York, it is a pleasant contrast to some of the airports here. As of right now (February 2024), they still haven't added the airport lounges, but I heard they should be coming online shortly. Good news.

# 3

# The Basics

Before we get started I would recommend downloading an app called "The Magic Of The Caribbean". The link is listed below. It will save you 10% on a lot of restaurants, activities, hotels etc in Saint Martin. I had no idea about this until the 3rd week of my stay. I was surprised the Airbnb host never mentioned this app as this would have saved me hundreds of $$. It costs $29 and lasts for an entire year. I would check on the site to see which hotels and restaurants participate in the program and if it is going to be worth it for you.

**magicofthecaribbean.com**

In addition, there are of course more things to do in Saint Martin than I will cover, but this book will go over my favorites (i.e. what I would do if I visited there, especially the first go around).

## SOME QUICK STATS

The total population of Saint Martin is about 74K (42K on the Dutch side, 32K on the French side). The biggest economic driver of the island is tourism (about 85% of the economy). About 1 million people visit Saint Martin every year (excluding the people who use Saint Martin in transit to another island like St. Barths or Anguilla).

## WHEN TO GO/WEATHER?

The high season runs from December to the end of April. Like many places, the very end of November to early mid-December has relatively reasonable pricing (versus the rest of the high season). Weather-wise, during this time, it is pretty awesome, ranging from mid-70s to mid-80s.

The low season is from May to the end of November. This is also the hottest time of the year and the wettest time. When I tell you, it is hot..I mean, it is HOT. I kept reading somewhere that it is around the same temperature all year round, but I personally did not find this to be the case. During the low season (summer), it got well into the 90s. This may be due to climate change, so possibly before, it was different, but currently, it is HOT in the summer. This is why I find most articles on Saint Martin more "touristy" than REAL. There is also a good amount of rain in the morning. In addition, there could be a decent amount of afternoon-evening thunderstorms. But it is much cheaper (about 50%-70% cheaper than the high season) than the rest of the year outside of hurricane season.

From September to November is the hurricane season. Not only does it rain a lot but lots of touristy places and hotels may be closed. I personally wouldn't visit during this time as even the other neighboring island are mainly closed as well so it likely won't be fun and vibrant. If you are looking to go and just be someplace completely quiet, you can get some accommodations on the very cheap, so this may work for you, but just warning you, lots of places will be closed i.e DEAD.

## OTHER MUST KNOW INFO

The currency is Euro, but $USD is usually accepted almost everywhere. Keep in mind lots of places only take cash (ie some ferries, etc.), so I would definitely keep some cash with you, although there are plenty of ATMs around as well in a pinch.

The "official" language on the Dutch side is Dutch, but I rarely heard people speaking Dutch, mainly English. I'm sure there are some "Dutch" speaking areas, but I never came across them on my travels there. The French side is a bit different. I hear French all over the place. For me, I loved it as I took some years of French and thought it was great I could put some of those years into practice. Everyone did also speak English so if you don't speak French, definitely don't sweat it. And almost everyone spoke English VERY well.

**To have a car/not have a car.** If you are staying at a resort and don't plan to leave much, then you probably don't need to rent a car, as cabs/taxis are very prevalent on this island. They are more on the expensive, though. I would recommend renting a car if you plan to visit. The island is pretty spread out, so it may take a while for you to get from one place to another, and it will cost you a lot (i.e., $60-$80) from your resort to someplace 30-40 minutes away one way. So not only was it more economical, but I found Saint Martin to be one of those places where lots of people actually "live," unlike, for example, Turks and Caicos, where the entire island feels like a big resort. So if you plan to hike, go to different parts of the island, and explore…renting a car for me was much better than not having one as it wasn't crazy expensive to rent a car ($50-60 per day). Plus, you have more control over your time.

Sidebar: If you are near Marigot area there are a lot of very fast, and somewhat "reckless" people on motorcycles doing wheelies (even at night) so when you are driving, just be aware and on the lookout for these bikers. There was several times when I was close to a collision because other people were not being careful. Just a heads up to be on your toes.

## TRAFFIC

This gets me to another topic that I wish someone had told me about when I got there. There is insane traffic in certain parts of the island during rush hour. This traffic can be comparable to New York City traffic or other highly congested areas that may drive you bananas. The last thing I wanted to do on vacation was sit in traffic for hours on end.

The worst traffic times are typically during the morning and late afternoon rush hours, around 8-9 AM and 4-6 PM. The worst areas during these times are Marigot and Philipsburg as well as the Simpson Bay area near the drawbridge (where traffic can be heavily delayed by bridge openings for boat traffic. It's wise to plan travel outside these peak times or explore alternative routes when possible). So be warned.

## GROCERIES

If you are staying for an extended period of time and want to get groceries, I would recommend The Super-U. They are super clean, nice, and a pleasant experience all around. You can get pretty much whatever you need there and they are all over the island.

In addition, there are many super quaint, beautiful little grocery stores (especially on the French side) where you can stock up on the most amazing food. In these little drop-in delis, you really understand that the food is not just food but an art.

# 4

# Orient Beach

This was my favorite part of the island, and I plan to stay in this area whenever I go back to Saint Martin. First of all the area is just nice, super quaint, very French, and charming. It felt like, at times, I was in a cute suburban area of Southern France. This area is about 35 minutes from SXM (Princess Juliana International Airport). This area also tends to be on the higher end of prices for accommodation/restaurant prices, probably because it is one of the most popular areas on the island. The food at every restaurant that I visited rivaled restaurants in New York City so ie FOOD IS REALLY GOOD in most restaurants in the area.

FYI, this is a windy beach. I ran into someone who traveled regularly to Orient Beach, and she said it was her favorite beach on the island, and it was beautiful and calm. I have been to Orient Bay Beach in both high and low seasons, and BOTH times, Orient Beach was windy. So, from my experience, you can't really swim around in the water without getting moved around a bit. If that bothers you, then you are better off finding another beach to swim and chill in. There is a reason why kite surfers are all over this beach. That's because there is a decent amount of wind. So Orient Beach is great for people-watching, hanging out at the best beach clubs on the island, a high concentration of incredible restaurants, reading a book on the beach, and a quaint/cute neighborhood, but a chill, swimmable experience is not one of them from my experience. You can definitely go in the water, body surf, but you probably will get tossed around somewhat.

There some really amazing beach clubs in this area. For me, they were my favorite beach clubs on the entire island. Just FYI many of the beach clubs are closed for dinner on most nights, so I would email/and or check on the website which nights they are open (depends on the season).

## COCO BEACH CLUB & RESTAURANT

## $$$ (expensive)

**cocobeach.restaurant**

**Parc de la Baie Orientale, Orient Bay Beach Saint Martin, 97150, Saint-Martin 97150, SAINT-MARTIN**

Just to warn you, this place gets busy during the high season, so I would make sure to call or email them to make a reservation. Entrees are about $30-$50. Drinks about $15-20.

I walked into this place and thought, "This is a vacation." It was beautiful and high-end. Just FYI, all beach clubs on the island WILL charge you to rent lounge chairs on the beach (if not affiliated with a hotel), and the price varies depending on the season, i.e., $25-30 for two chairs for high-season (unless they change the prices).

The food here was great. They also have live music and dancing on certain days/nights. Coco Beach serves lunch daily and dinner mainly on weekends, but I would check the site when they are exactly open for dinner as it changes with the season.

Food and drinks are great here and was one of my favorite spots on the island. So I have no hesitation recommending this place.

## KKO BEACH BAR & RESTAURANT

**$$$ (moderately expensive)**

**Plage de la Baie Orientale, Saint Martin 97150, St. Martin**

**kkobeach.com**

This restaurant is right next door to Coco Beach. I loved this restaurant as it reminded me of the chill, beautiful beach clubs in Greece. The food is great, like the rest of the restaurants in the Orient Beach area. The vibe is a bit more chill.

One thing I would note is that when you are ordering and ask for anything "extra," they may charge you. For example, I ordered scrambled eggs and asked them to add some tomatoes. They charged me extra for tomatoes. I had never been to a restaurant where they charged for adding spinach or tomatoes to an omelet or eggs but apparently this restaurant does (and the additional was $7, which I thought was a bit overboard), but apparently that's what they said the policy.

With that being said, the view, the vibe were worth it.

This restaurant is affiliated with the Orient Beach Hotel. So, a continental breakfast is included in the stay. This boutique hotel is located right behind the restaurant and has great views of the beach right from your room. The beach chairs are also included in the stay, BUT not the first row. So, if you want to sit right in the right, you will have to pay a bit more.

## LA PLAYA ORIENT BAY HOTEL

**$$$ (moderately expensive)**

**116, Parc de la Baie Orientale, Orient Bay 97150, St. Martin**

**en.laplayaorientbay.com**

This is another beach hotel right on Orient Bay. It is beautiful and also has a great restaurant and bar. One thing I didn't like was when I hung out there, the music was too "clubbish" for my taste, but some people may not mind or even like that, so if that's your vibe, then go for it. It's another great beach club in the area.

## BIKINI BEACH

$$-$$$(It is in between moderate and moderate expensive)

**bikinibeach.restaurant**

This restaurant is not affiliated with a hotel. This is more of a chiller vibe but still has the feeling of being upscale and nice. They serve breakfast, lunch, and dinner, but dinner is more of a limited menu. Again, the food and drinks, like the rest, were great. I would say this is the chillest of the beach clubs I have mentioned.

## ORIENT VILLAGE

**The Orient Bay Village is one of my favorite parts of Saint Martin.** It is the adorable collection of eight amazing, restaurants nestled near the beach. The variety and food quality is incredible. They have sushi,

French, Italian, seafood, traditional American, and the most incredible gelato Place I have ever been to.

The restaurant is called **The Treasures of The Caribbean** and was started by a famous TWO star Michelin Celebrity Chef from Montreal named Jerome Ferrer. His restaurant in Montreal was voted THE BEST restaurant in Canada in 2018 and now he has graced Orient Bay with his incredible and the most eclectic assortment of gelato I have ever seen. You will find unusual and beautiful flavors here like Rosewater Mint Gelato, Sea Salt Caramel, and Pretzel, that you won't find anywhere else. And they are made from complete scratch in the back.

Chef Ferrer commutes from Montreal to Saint Martin every month, and when he is in Saint Martin, he has a five-course tasting menu that is probably the best value on the island. It's 50 Euros for a five-course menu from a TWO star Michelin chef. How much better can you get than that?? And for dessert (which is included with the five-course menu), you get UNLIMITED gelato. If you are lucky enough to be there when he creates his five course menu...book it. The food and the presentation is a very cool experience. Needless to say it was one of BEST food experiences I have ever had...and only in Saint Martin!

# 5

# La Samanna Hotel

$$$$ (expensive)

**Baie Longue Terres Basses Saint Martin, 97064, St. Martin**

**belmond.com/hotels/north-america/caribbean/st-martin/belmond-la-samanna**

If you are able to…you MUST have lunch at La Samanna. It is simply gorgeous, the views are breathtaking, the beach is sublime, and La Samanna is deserving the high price tag per night. Hands down, it is the best luxury hotel on the island by a big margin. The hotel is part of the Luxury Hotel Brand The Belmont. Any hotel part of this group is of the highest caliber.

One thing to note is the Hotel does close during some of the low season, so contact the hotel to see when you can visit if you are planning any time in the low season.

Make a lunch reservation at Laplaj Restaurant and I promise you, you will be very happy you did.

Have drinks and watch the sunset at the Baie Lounge Bar. It is probably the best sunset view on the island.

# 6

# Hiking In Paradise

## Pic Paradis

For breathtaking view of the island Pic Paradis is an awesome place to hike to. Pic Paradis is the highest point on the island and offers trails through beautiful back country.

It's a paradise for hikers.

# Hikes to Pic Paradis

The trails around Pic Paradis offer something for everyone. The trails go from easy to challenging, with each providing unique views and environments. Depending on your physical endurance level and hiking preferences, you can choose from several trails, each offering a different perspective of Saint Martin's. There are varying trails to the top, so I'm going to break it down in terms of difficulty.

## <u>EASY</u>

**<u>West Coast (Kim Sha) Trail:</u>** If you're looking for an easier hike, the West Coast Trail is an excellent choice. This trail is about 2.4 miles one way and is considered more of a leisurely hike. This trail offers a mix of natural beauty and local life. Time-wise, it's approximately 1 hour and 30 minutes for a round trip.

The West Coast Trail begins at Kimsha Beach and ends at Mullet Bay in St. Martin. The West Coast Kim Sha trail features restaurants, bars, yachts, historic buildings, and hotels, which are visible as hikers journey past Simpson Bay Lagoon over the Simpson Bay drawbridge. The journey also takes hikers past Simpson Bay Beach, the upscale residential area of Beacon Hill, and Maho Beach, where many people enjoy watching the plane landings at Princess Juliana International Airport.

Some of the plant life that can be seen along the West Coast Kim Sha hiking trail include coconut palms, beach morning glory, and sea grape trees along the sandy beaches. The wildlife that can be seen along the West Coast Trail from Kim Sha includes shore birds and different kinds of sea turtles such as the leatherback, hawksbill, and green sea turtle. The round-trip hike along this hiking trail is at least 1 hour and 30 minutes long.

## MODERATE/MODERATE DIFFICULT

Pic Paradis Trail from Loterie Farm: This trail is considered moderate, stretching approximately 2.8 miles roundtrip. It usually takes about 2.5 to 3 hours to complete, factoring in time for photo stops. This hike offers amazing views and the opportunity to encounter diverse wildlife. **The entry to Loterie Farm is 10 euros**, and they provide a map for guidance. The hike includes steep switchbacks, a rock scramble section, and requires an elevation gain of over 1,100 feet. This trail is mostly shaded, making it a bit more comfortable in terms of temperature, and it leads you through beautiful forested areas to stunning viewpoints, including the famous Chewbacca Viewpoint.

## BACK BAY: Hiking To A Natural Pool

DON'T FORGET WATER SHOES, SUNBLOCK AND TOWELS IF YOU PLAN TO GO INTO THE NATURAL POOL!

## MODERATE

Located on the East coast of the island, Back Bay and Geneva Bay are accessible via a path either from Guana Bay or from Point Blanche, two upper middle class neighborhoods.

Starting the hike to the natural pool is the easiest and shortest from Pointe Blanche (20 minutes) but if you want a longer hike (about an hour) then start at Guana Bay. I would bring water shoes if you plan to take a dip in the natural pool.

The 20 minute hike will take you along a small path and some steep cliffs with waters below. You will likely see some pelicans and iguanas soaking up the sun along this route.

You should finally get to a beautiful pool below which looks like diamonds shining in the light.

I would suggest leaving earlier in the day to beat the high heat.

The trail runs closely to the edge of rocky cliffs and there is always the possibility of sliding on small rocks or tripping on one. Caution needs to be heeded at all times.

The short version of the Back Bay hike from Point Blanche, like the longer version starting from Guana Bay is stunning.

## REMEMBER THE BASICS

**Start Early:** Begin your hike early in the morning to avoid the midday heat, especially if this is during the late spring or summer. This also gives you the best chance to see wildlife and to take in the views before any potential afternoon clouds roll in.

**Wear Proper Gear:** Ensure you're wearing comfortable, sturdy hiking shoes, as the trails can be rocky and uneven. Bring a hat, sunscreen, and insect repellent to protect against the sun and bugs.

**Stay Hydrated and Pack Snacks:** Carry enough water to stay hydrated throughout the hike, and bring snacks or a picnic to enjoy at the summit. There are NO facilities on the trails, so you'll need to bring everything you might need.

**Don't Forget Your Camera/Bring a phone charger:** Make sure your camera or phone is charged and ready to capture the beautiful scenery.

**Be Respectful of Nature:** Stay on marked trails to protect the island's natural habitats and wildlife. Take all your trash with you to keep the area pristine for future visitors.

**Consider a Guide:** If you're unfamiliar with the area or prefer not to hike alone, consider hiring a local guide who can provide insights into the flora, fauna, and history of the region.

# 7

# Rainforest Adventures

***THE FLYING DUTCHMAN***

**rainforestadventure.com**

**LB Scott Rd #39, Cul de Sac, Sint Maarten**

Rainforest Adventures is an eco-adventure park located on Rockland Estate (a former sugar plantation).

If you love rides you are going to love Rainforest Adventures. I recommend booking ahead of time and seeing if they are offering any extra discounts. YOU PROBABLY WANT TO CALL AHEAD AND SEE HOW LONG THE WAIT IS. Sometimes the wait can be REALLY long, especially with all the cruises (ie the wait can be up to 3-6 hours long if it gets really packed which is ridiculous, so check beforehand). If it's during a really busy time I would probably pass on this as in my opinion, no ride is worth a 3-6 hour wait.

If it is not a big cruise day then I think it is a very fun and memorable excursion! One thing to note, even though the website says it is for the whole family, the rides aren't appropriate for small children

Rainforest Adventures has the steepest zip line in the world called the Flying Dutchman (although be prepared to walk up some stairs). The views are beautiful and the ride is awesome. The best way to go is to book the Big Three Full Experience which includes the chairlift, the slide, and all the zip lines. Don't forget sunblock!

**They have six activities:**

**1) Emilio Wilson Museum** = It is an interesting museum that shows what life was like on a plantation. You also learn about the customs, traditions, and history of Saint Martin. It was fine but nothing extraordinary but still educational and great overview.

**2) Sentry Hill Zipline/Sky Explorer/Sentry Hill View** = These two activities (plus the view at the top of Sentry Hill) are combined on one ticket as the Sky Explorer is a chair lift that takes you up giving you an amazing 360-degree view of Saint Martin and the Sentry Hill Zipline flies you over the mountain range. Then you strap back on the Sky Explorer on the way down. The chairlift is slow in my opinion but the views are great. Sentry Hill is one of the highest points on the island and you can see parts of Anguilla, St. Barths, Statia, and Saba. The zip line experience is fast (about 30 seconds). I'm mixed on this experience as both the ride up and down was slow but zip line quick.

*SKY EXPLORER*

**3) The Flying Dutchman** = This is the best experience at Rainforest Adventures (if the wait isn't ridiculous) and a must-do. I would recommend not wearing anything on your face that could fly off ie sunglasses. Even though it is the steepest zip line in the world, it isn't as scary as it sounds (well if you aren't afraid of heights) and was such a blast. Keep your eyes open as the views are astounding and it goes by fast. The ride is about 45 seconds long at a speed of 40 mph. You also take the chairlift up (about 30 minutes) but again the views are amazing.

*Schooner Ride*

**4) The Schooner Ride** = This ride for me was just OK. It is an inter-tube ride (dry) down a hill. The ride was bumpy and you get turned around.

## Emilio's Restaurant

This is the owner's former plantation house and is at the base of the zip line area. Food and drinks are great so would HIGHLY recommend this place to grab food or drinks. This restaurant is also highly rated so it's great to have some eco-adventure fun and then head to restaurant for food and drinks. You can book reservations from the link below. The restaurant consistently gets ranked as a "top choice" on Tripadvisor.

In 1954, Emilio Wilson, the grandson of a former slave, bought the entire area/ surrounding property and opened it to the public as a park in memory of the slaves who made St. Martin what it was.

https://emilios-sxm.com/

*Emilio's Restaurant*

# 8

# Pinel Island

*View of Pinel*

*KARIBUNI RESTAURANT (On Pinel Island)*

**lekaribuni.com/hotel** (hotel is on St. Martin while the Restaurant is on Pinel)

**Lot 29 les terrasses de cul de sac Saint Martin, 97150, St. Martin**

Pinel is another one of my favorite spots in the Saint Martin area. This beautiful sandbar island is just a five-minute boat ride from Saint Martin.

You can catch the public boat at Cul de Sac. You will see a big sign for the public boat that leaves every 30 minutes (except if the weather won't allow it). The "boat" is more like a large rowboat and costs about 10-12 Euros each way. The boat road is short and lovely. The last boat leaves Pinel at 5 pm ET daily (**so you better catch it**).

***PUBLIC BOAT TO PINEL***

If you are staying at Karibuni Hotel in the Cul de Sac area on Saint Martin, they have a private boat that will take you back and forth to Pinel. In addition, they have complimentary beach chairs they will set up for you on the island. Pinel Beach on the Karibuni Restuarant side is the official "beach" of the hotel, hence why they have complimentary chairs on Pinel.

The Karibuni Restaurant on Pinel is also the official restaurant of the hotel (again the hotel is NOT on the island but the official restaurant and the beach is). The restaurant is awesome, the food is delicious, and the vibe is quaint and tropical. I REALLY felt like I was on vacation at the restaurant. They have lobster you can pick straight from the cage in the ocean. The poke bowl was the best I have ever had. You can order your food/drinks directly from the beach chairs or sit at the really cute restaurant.

If you are renting chairs/umbrellas on Pinel (and not a guest of the hotel) it will cost you ~ $20pp on the Karibuni Restaurant side and about the same Yellow Beach side. Yellow Beach is a tad windier than the Karibuni side by only by a small margin. Both sides are beautiful, chill and fun.

The Yellow Beach is right next door to the Karibuni Restaurant and also has amazing food and drinks. BOTH restaurants have stand-up tables right in the water so you can have drinks and food while part of your body is in the crystal-clear blue water.

*YELLOW BEACH PINEL*

*stand up tables in water*

If you feel a bit adventurous you can also rent a kayak to get to Pinel and back. I personally didn't do that as you never know how the weather will be when you row back and you have to keep track of your kayak when you get to Pinel. I saw a couple of times when people had to chase their kayak and grab it as it drifted back into the water.

Renting a kayak is about $30pp for the day which is pretty affordable. I still would recommend it if you are looking to get some exercise and the weather is clear. It takes about 20-25 minutes each way if you are kayaking. Again, if you plan to do this, then be mindful of the weather and season as I have seen it get pretty windy and that could be a struggle kayaking back and forth.

One of the things I love about Pinel is the beach. As you can see from the first picture, the sand is white, and the sandbar is beautiful, the water is calm and stunning.

# 9

# Sail To Tintamarre

**tintamarreexpress.com** ..website for shuttle service (RT $25pp/ under 6 free). This website can also do snorkeling trips to the island.

Tintamarre is a deserted island just two miles north of Saint Martin. You can only get there by boat. It is only about 250 acres and is part of a natural preserve.

You can either take a shuttle (about 15 minutes to cross), or hire a private boat or there are lots of group excursions you can sign up for (with or without meals). You can also rent a kayak which will take you about an hour each way.

Tintamarre is famous for its turquoise deserted beach and untouched nature vibe. You can swim on the beautiful beach in front of gorgeous red cliffs. You won't see any restaurants or set up-beach chairs here. It is just clean, pure untamed nature. It is an amazing snorkeling spot and you will likely see some turtles and stingrays around. There is also a shipwreck you can check out with snorkeling.

Remember, if you are taking the shuttle or kayaking, make sure to bring water, food or whatever you may need because you will not be able to buy necessities on the island. In addition there are NO pets allowed into the Nature Reserve.

# 10

# Loterie Farm

**loteriefarm.com**

## Rue du Pic Paradis, St Martin 97150, St Martin

I would call Loterie Farm an outdoor eco-adventure spa, tropical sanctuary and restaurant. It is complete with zip lines, hiking, various pools, cabanas, and a treehouse restaurant. You can spend your entire day here. One thing I would note is that I personally would avoid the weekends. This sanctuary turns into somewhat of a loud club which isn't my vibe but if that's your thing then go for it. You will see a decent amount of Insta-posers here. I went here on a Saturday afternoon and it felt like a busy loud Miami club...the exact opposite of what I was looking for in an eco-spa sanctuary so if you are truly looking for peace then I would advise going on a weekday.

They have a beautiful pool area where you can just hang out and be surrounded by nature. This place is literally in the middle of the jungle. After hanging out in the pools (there are more than one), you can move over to the tree house-looking restaurant where they have drinks, tapas, and full or four-course meals. Reservations for the "Jungle Room Restaurant" can be made on Open Table.

*JUNGLE ROOM RESTAURANT*

If you are looking for something more active, there is the hike to Pic Paradis, as we mentioned in a previous chapter, but they also have zip lining through the jungle.

They will actually teach you how to harness and strap yourself. You are going to be zipping from tree to tree but on your own. You will be surrounding by the sounds of monkeys and birds while zipping yourself through the jungle.

*ZIPLINING*

Reminder: you can't wear open-toed shoes, i.e., no sandals, so bring tennis or hiking shoes, and if you have long hair, you need to put your hair in a pony tail.

There is also a "kids adventure park" with a kiddie pool and jungle gym. It costs 20 euros per child, and one parent can bring up to two children.

# 11

# Grand Case

So when I first got to the Grand Case area, I found it a bit strange. On one hand, it was a beautiful beach area. The water was blue, calm, and clear, and the sand white with amazing restaurants. On the other hand, parts of the area was completely run down, and looked sketchy and some of it looked like a war zone. Clearly much of the area still hadn't recovered from Irma. So I am a bit torn about this area. If you don't wander into the road and just look from the beach, it looks great. That was my first impression of the area...a mixed bag.

So, given that, I did find some really great spots.

**Grand Case Beach Club**

At the very end was a cute little hotel toward the very end. We stayed here a few times. It's a nice, quaint hotel that seemed to be a bit detached from the more chaotic center of Grand Case. For us, it was peaceful and just what we were looking for. The water was gorgeous, the restaurant had great food, and you could even snorkel right at the beach and see lots of amazing fish.

### Rainbow Cafe

We loved this restaurant. It was like Karibuni, or a chill restaurant that you would see in Orient Beach or in St. Barths. Food and drinks was great. And look at that view of the beach!

It does get booked up, so I would make a reservation beforehand. This was a solid and relaxing quaint spot in Grand Case.

## Ocean 82

This was one of our favorite restaurants in Saint Martin. They have glass all around the restaurant so you can see clear into the water. They always sat us right next to the water, so we had the most gorgeous views, especially at sunset. If you do plan to eat here for sunset, then I would make a reservation and ask specifically to be seated right next to the water. The service, food, and drinks were all amazing. This is why this restaurant became one of our go-to's.

# 12

# Day To Saint Barths

**DON'T FORGET YOUR PASSPORT** (when you are going to any of the neighboring islands outside of Pinel and Tintamarre). Do not forget to bring your documents. You are entering another territory, so you will need your passport or will NOT be able to travel. **IN ADDITION,**

**there are departure TAXES** (around $10) that need to be paid in cash when traveling by boat. If you are traveling by plane, the departure tax is already included in your price.

St. Barths is my favorite Caribbean island. I find it to be unlike anywhere else. First of all, it's a quick trip from the US East Coast. It's beautiful, yet overall safe and still retains it's natural beauty. It is also very expensive, but I think it's worth the hype. The water is the most perfect temperature, and the scenery is gorgeous. The weather is perfect almost all year round. Because it's a French territory, St. Barts has this chic, French vibe going for it. So if you want a day trip or stay overnight here go for it. It's like getting a slice of the French Riviera in the Caribbean.

The island is all about providing stellar service and ensuring privacy for its visitors. This means amazing resorts, villas, gourmet restaurants, and boutique shopping. Plus, since the island is often attracts a wealthy, exclusive and sometimes celebrity clientele, the businesses on the island go out of their way to make sure you're getting the peace and quiet you're paying for.

**Just don't go from mid-August to the end of October.** It is absolutely dead during that time and most things are closed.

If you plan ahead you can get a "decent" price for a flight from St. Martin to St. Barths. What I mean by decent is, about $280 round trip. Since the planes generally only seat about 6-10 people, flights are still going to be relatively expensive for a 15-minute flight, but it is a really cool experience. The famous St. Barths runway is beautiful to see as it lands right near the turquoise water.

The ferry ride is also a nice experience. The total commute time on the ferry is about 45 minutes.

**CALL AHEAD OF EMAIL TO SEE SCHEDULE/RATES DURING DIFFERENT SEASONS.**

The **Great Bay Express** is the fastest boat to Saint Barths departing from Philipsburg. The service runs about three times a day in peak season. Round trip (Day trip) is about 56 Euros. Round trip (non-day trip) is about 90 Euros.

**greatbayexpress.com**

A second company, **Voyager**, operates from the French side of Marigot and takes about 60 minutes. It also runs about three times per day in peak season. Same-day round trip is 72 Euros, and open ticket round trip is 92 Euros.

**voy12.com**

*landing on the St. Barths famous runway by small plane*

What I love about St. Barths is that the island is very very clean, and the landscape is just gorgeous. I would highly recommend renting a car to drive all around the island. You can do that online and pick the car right up at the airport. The airport itself is tiny, so its really convenient to pick up your car.

St. Jean Beach is probably the most famous beach in St. Barths. This is the beach where you can just hang out and watch the small planes land on the strip. It's always a super fun experience.

St Jeans Beach is also where the famous hotel Eden Roc is. Just like almost everywhere is St.Barths, it is very expensive, but if you want to splurge, you can make reservations directly at the Sand Bar for lunch or dinner. The beach lounge chairs directly on the beach are only for hotel guests, but we were able to use the lounge chairs sometimes during the non-peak season when we made reservations at the Sand Bar Restaurant...but that was only at the discretion of the restaurant.

*SAND BAR RESTAURANT EDEN ROC HOTEL*

On the same beach, just farther down, there is a much more chill, quaint restaurant hotel called Pearl Beach Hotel. They do rent beach lounges for about 35-50 Euros pp (depending on the season). In general, renting beach chairs in St Barths compared to St Martin will be about 3-4X the price.

*PEARL BEACH HOTEL*

*GUSTAVIA*

Gustavia is the capital of this tiny island, and you will find the best high-end shopping on three main roads: Quai de la Republique, Rue du General de Gaulle, and Rue de Roi Oscar 11.

The popular harbour-side street of Quai de la République features a solid lineup of designer stores such as Louis Vuitton, Dior, and Hermès, some holding items you won't find elsewhere in the world.

*SHOPPING IN GUSTAVIA*

You can also continue your search for designer stores and explore the nearby Carré d'Or plaza and the Coeur Vendôme Center, for further designers like Roberto Cavalli, Ralph Lauren, and Prada.

*LE TOINY BEACH CLUB*

If you want to visit a quieter side of the island I would suggest going to have lunch at Le Toiny Beach Club. The hotel is absolutely gorgeous, and there will be a car at reception to take you down to the beautiful, rustic restaurant right on the beach.

## HOW DID ST BARTHS BECOME AN EXCLUSIVE GO TO GLOBAL VACATION SPOT?

St. Barts started to become famous around the 1950s and 1960s. The real turning point came when David Rockefeller (the US business mogul) bought a property there in the 1950s. This purchase was like a giant spotlight on St. Barts, signaling to the world's wealthy and famous that this little island was the place to be.

Before this high-profile purchase, St. Barts was pretty much a well-kept secret, known mainly for its tough life and hardworking people, without much in the way of natural resources or industry. It was the quintessential sleepy, beautiful island with not much going on economically.

Rockefeller's investment started a trend. Soon, other wealthy individuals and celebrities began flocking to the island, drawn by its beauty, privacy, and the luxurious lifestyle it promised. These high-profile visitors brought attention to the island, and word of mouth did its magic. Over time, the island developed its infrastructure to cater to this upscale clientele, with luxury villas, gourmet restaurants, and chic boutiques popping up to meet the demand.

The island had the charm and beauty all along; it just needed that initial celebrity endorsement to put it on the map.

# 13

# BEACHES

***MAHO BEACH***

While there are so many beaches to talk about in St Martin, I am only going to highlight a couple here that I think are unique.

Unlike St. Jeans Beach in St. Barths where you watch small planes land on the strip, Maho Beach in St Martin is where you can watch the large commercial airplanes land and take off from the International Airport.

Sunset Bar and Grill is right on the beach and is probably the most popular spot to watch planes land and take off from the airport while you grab food and drinks.

**HAPPY BAY BEACH**

The most notable thing about Happy Bay Beach is that, it is the go-to nude beach on the island. While beaches on the French side allow going topless, Happy Bay is the most famous nude beach on the island, as it is also more secluded. It is a place where you can take a nap and is less "touristy." About roughly half of the people on the beach were nude, and total nudity seemed acceptable.

Happy Bay Beach is hidden, fairly untouched, and can only be accessible by boat or hiking. You can park your car at Friar's Bay and then walk to the end of the beach where the trail to Happy Bay starts (which is only about 20 20-minute walk).

You will find the closed gate with "Happy Bay" spray painted on it, walk around the gate and up the paved road. When the pavement turns right, continue straight on the dirt road down to the beach. There are NO chairs or umbrellas to rent, so if you want some shade, you need to bring your own stuff (like towels, etc). There is a small bar there as well (cash only).

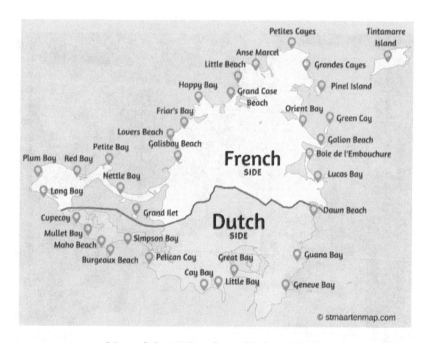

*Map of the 37 Beaches of Saint Martin*

We tried a bunch of beaches including Mullet Bay, Friar's Bay, Simpson and Anse Marcel (which was really far from most places) and we found that we would much rather spend the day at Pinel Island than go to the busier beaches on St. Martin. That was just our preference though but many people we talked to loved Mullet and Simpson Bay the best out of all the beaches on the island for swimming and chilling out.

Don't get me wrong, both Mullet and Simpson Bay had beautiful water but we preferred the "detachment" into nature of Pinel Island. But out of all the very swimmable beaches, Mullet and Simpson Bay are a solid bet. Again we loved the Orient Bay Beach area but we found the beach to be a bit more on the windy side.

*Kalatua Beach Club*

Kalatua Beach Club

$$$ (moderate)

kalatua.com

If you are in Mullet Bay we found a great beach club called Kalatua Beach Club. We found this one to be the best on the beach. Great food, drinks and vibe. Just know like a lot of beach clubs on the island, they are mainly "day" clubs and close around sunset. I would make sure to make reservations as they can get really booked up, especially around the busy season.

I asked about why they didn't stay open later. They said mosquitoes were the main reason as they come out in full force on the beach at night but to me that really didn't make sense as many other islands stay open into the night with the same mosquito problem. I didn't find St. Martin to be more mosquito-y than other islands (although still annoying) but I didn't buy that mosquitoes were the reason but who knows.

*Mullet Bay*

Just FYI there is a golf course in Mullet Bay near the beach but it is one of the most neglected golf courses I have ever seen so in my opinion, don't bother.

*Simpson Bay*

Anse Marcel beach is also beautiful but it was far from the airport (about 45 minutes away and $80 cab ride from airport each way ) and other centers of activity and is more remote. Also you have to drive on big hill to get to the area that many taxis don't like to go on as they could get stuck there in the rain which can be a pain for them. But if you don't mind the distance and want to step away from the world it's a fine spot.

*Anse Marcel Beach*

# 14

# LAYOVER/STOPOVER PARADISE

*The Morgan Resort*

themorganresort.com

If you are anything like me, I find long layovers brutal so hence why I am highlighting Morgan Resort. If you happen to check out of your hotel but your flight is much later, and you need to kill some time, or you are coming from another island, and your flight to your final destination is much later, then consider chilling out with a day pass at the Morgan Resort.

It is just one mile from the International Airport (SXM), and there is even a free shuttle to the airport. It's $50 for a day pass, and you can use all the hotel facilities, including the pool, jacuzzi, Wi-Fi, and restaurants. I'd much rather take a nap lounging next to the pool, getting served food and drinks, than wait for hours in an airport. The hotel is modern, clean, and chill, with beautiful water views and is right next to the airport.

# 15

# EXTRAS

## FINE DINING

Travel and Leisure cited in 2022 that Saint Martin is now the culinary capital of the Caribbean. This was one of the best surprises when visiting the island. Some of the food was really next-level. We have been all over the Caribbean, Turks and Caicos, The Bahamas, Anguilla, and St. Barths, in addition to New York City (where we live), Paris, London, Hong Kong, San Fran, etc., and some of the restaurants in St. Martin were up there with the best in the world. I would have to say the BEST restaurants in Saint Martin were better than the BEST we went to in Anguilla and St. Barths.

### THE VILLA HIBISCUS

$$$$ (expensive)

*Villa Hibiscus*

We had a chance to eat one of the best dinners we have ever had. This was at Villa Hibiscus. The Villa Hibiscus is a small, quaint hotel with only six rooms (all individually decorated). Although the rooms are absolutely lovely, it's the restaurant that gets the most attention.

Eating at Villa Hibiscus will take your culinary experience to an entirely new level. The hotel restaurant is perched under the shadows of Pic Paradis which is the highest point on St. Martin. It is owned and operated by chef Bastien Schenk and his wife Sabine. Schenk trained under Joêl Robuchon back in France, before moving back to the childhood home of his wife. Together, they create a tasting menu that could compete with the best in the world. This is all while you overlook the entirety of the island spilling out into the Caribbean Sea below. Not to mention, the entire restaurant feels like a dreamy home, not a stuffy restaurant.

We also had the privilege of touring the immaculate kitchen. I often expect restaurant kitchens to be chaotic, but this one was calm and zen-like. Each dish was like a work of art.

**L'Oursin Restaurant (La Samanna Hotel)**

$$$$ (expensive)

IIn my opinion, this is not only a 5 star restaurant but has the BEST views on the island.

This restaurant was voted the Best Hotel Restaurant on Saint Martin. The food is beautiful, and amazing, the staff is attentive. Although the prices are expensive it is worth it.

*L'Oursin*

*L'Oursin*

*L'Atelier (located in Orient Bay Village)*

*L'Atelier*

## L'Atelier

latelier-sxm.com

$$ (moderate)

I wanted to point this one out because I walked past it and it is just a cozy vacation-esque adorable French little bar/bistro in Orient Bay Village. As I mentioned before we really didn't need to leave Orient Bay because so much of what we liked was there. Cute French vibe, and tons of amazing restaurants and beach clubs. The food at L'Atelier is absolutely outstanding and this restaurant is up there on top of my foodie list. It is hands down one of the best restaurants on the island in my opinion.

# OTHER EXCURSIONS

*Topper's Rhum Distillery*

*Topper's Rhum Distillery*

*Rhum Tasting Room*

## Topper's Rhum Distillery

60 Welfare Rd, Cole Bay, Sint Maarten

toppersrhumtours.com

I am just being honest. I am not a big drinker BUT I do love to watch how things are made. If either drinking rhum or watching how things are created is up your alley then this is a good spot to hit up. The tour guides are multi-lingual. Not only are there rhum samples but also rhum and pineapple cakes. There is also a bar, restaurant, and a gelato selection.

This tour is fun and educational. You learn about the history of rhum, and how Topper's started and it's super interactive.

This tour consistently gets really high ratings so it's an interesting excursion even if you aren't a big rhum drinker.

# 16

# MAP OF SAINT MARTIN

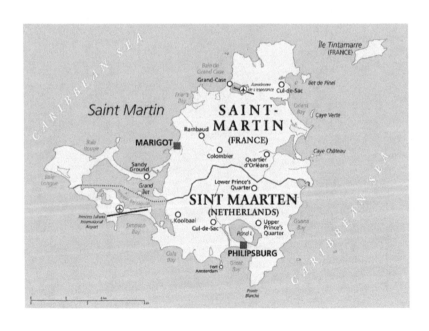